IMAGES
of England

NORMANTON
THE SECOND SELECTION

E. TIPPEY

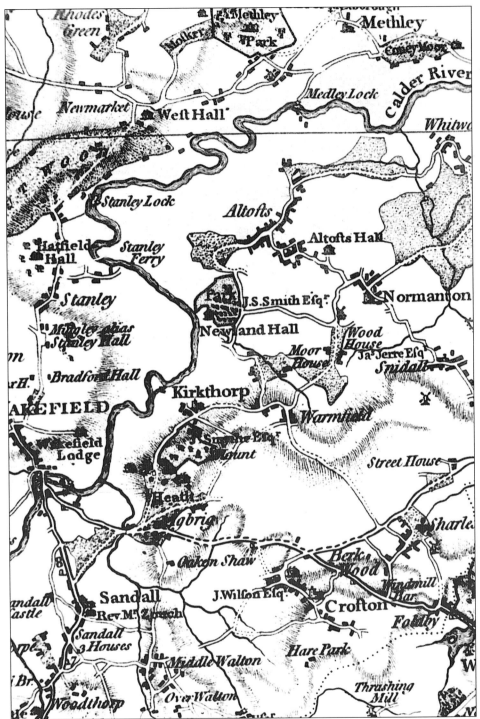

A map of the Normanton area in the eighteenth century, prior to the coming of the railway which started Normanton's boom. Although the church was in Normanton, Altofts at that time had a slightly bigger population of around 400. This was possible due to the small boatbuilding industry that was established around Shipcorner.

IMAGES
of England

NORMANTON
THE SECOND SELECTION

Compiled by
Bryan Fraser

TEMPUS

First published 2001
Copyright © Bryan Fraser, 2001

Tempus Publishing Limited
The Mill, Brimscombe Port,
Stroud, Gloucestershire, GL5 2QG

ISBN 0 7524 2296 0

Typesetting and origination by
Tempus Publishing Limited
Printed in Great Britain by
Midway Colour Print, Wiltshire

This early twentieth-century greetings postcard illustrates some of the changes that have taken place in Altofts. The Diamond Pit has gone, as have many of the houses, the gas lights on Church Road, and the Village Board offices at the entrance to the cemetery.

Contents

Acknowledgements

Once again may I thank the people of Normanton, without whose help by suppling memories and photographs, this book would have not been possible. Your memories are so important to local history, but even more important to your future generations. For many hundreds of years family passed on their history mostly by word of mouth. In today's world of mass communications, families are not passing on their history, and yet we have so many ways to record it for their future generations.

Finally may I specially thank Derek Auty and Joe Pratt for their help with this volume.

For these Altofts ladies and their children on this wagonette, the only outing they might get throughout the summer was a ride to a local park or beauty spot, such as Pontefract, Roundhay Park or Wetherby. They were determined to enjoy the day and its planning would have taken many weeks.

Introduction

Today's Normanton is the result of an amalgamation in 1938 of the two towns of Altofts and Normanton. At the time of that amalgamation, Altofts with the West Riding Colliery within its boundaries had money in the bank, while Normanton with none of the large collieries on its boundaries actually within the town's borders, was heavily in debt. However the town still had to supply the basic facilities for the many workers at those collieries who lived in the town.

Little is known of the early history of the area, but physical evidence exists of a Bronze Age settlement, overlooking the river at Birkwood in Altofts. The hill in Normanton park was possibly part of the Roman signalling system. Saxon dwellings were discovered when the Swan public house was first built and recently Saxon remains were also discovered on the former Normanton Golf Course.

The *Domesday Book* in 1086 mentions a priest and a church so Normanton must have been a flourishing village at the time. Altofts and Normanton remained two small villages for almost the next 800 years, until that great railway pioneer George Stephenson decided that the north-south line he was building would come through Normanton. Within a year lines from east and west joined that north-south line at Normanton and more people worked at Normanton station than had lived in the town a few years earlier. The first major postal sorting office in the north was established at Normanton station. The small shelter that remains on the station today is a sad reflection of its former splendour.

This railway junction enabled the rich coal seams in the Normanton area to be exploited. Within a few years over 10,000 men worked in the collieries around Normanton, only a few miles from its centre. These mines included at one stage the two most productive colliery complexes in Europe. Strongly patriotic, the miners volunteered in their thousands during the First World War and were killed in their hundreds. In this book we remember their sacrifice. Once again we look how Normanton has changed even since my first book, and how its people changed with it. The boom is now long over; the collieries have long gone, although a few Normanton men are still employed in the Selby coalfield. Normanton now has a variety of industries that exploit not the canal or railway but the motorway that runs through its boundaries. Some of the community spirit that was built up by the dangers of working in the local mines still remains. More and more of the town's people work in the nearby cities of Wakefield and Leeds. Many of the religious establishments built with money freely subscribed by the town's people who had little to give, if not closed already, are struggling to remain open. What little free time was available away from the pressure of financing and keeping large families, was spent in quiet enjoyment and often in helping good causes. Large working committees were organized to arrange charity events. The people responded by attending most of these in their thousands. Now most enjoyment is found in the television or computer.

This is now my fifth book on Normanton. I little dreamed when I started my research over twenty years ago that this would be possible. My research has been like a treasure hunt and occasionally the stories I have slowly pieced together have been my treasures. Some finds are already in print, some still need the final piece. My collection of photographs was started because of my desire to save what I considered was important for local history, and through the conviction that along with people's memories, they were important to save: once they have been lost, they are lost forever.

I have always referred to local history like a jigsaw, and each family who has lived in the town as a piece in that jigsaw. Sometimes the family has a large area and maybe one person in the family supplies a large piece. Occasionally a local person has a part in the jigsaw of national history. People from Normanton have made their mark on the country and international scene; people from my collection of photographs have gone on to represent their country or have been nationally known. Normanton people have settled throughout the world. This is shown by the variety of countries to which my books have been sent. As modern transport and communication seem to shrink the world, the need to safeguard our identity, our personal history, becomes more important.

My collection of photographs will eventually join other items I have deposited at Wakefield's local history archive, on permanent loan. There almost certainly it will be available on the World Wide Web so descendants of Normanton people all over the world can view and retrieve photographs of Normanton and its people and other information. How things have changed in twenty years!

Bryan Fraser
August 2001

Carnival Day on Castleford Road. Floats like this one – called 'Sing a Song of Sixpence' – would have taken many hours to complete. Activities like this gave comradeship and pride to all concerned.

One
Normanton Expands

Normanton's population up to the coming of the railway in 1840 was less than 400. The residents were grouped around the parish church, with another small community at Woodhouse, and various farm cottages. The sheep road from Castleford passed through and on, via Kirkthorpe, to the market at Wakefield.

Altofts at that time had just a few cottages and the occasional large house dotted along Church Road up to Birkwood Farm. This branched at Shipcorner to go via Altofts Hall to Normanton. The other road at that time went to Newland Hall, and not via Stanley Ferry to Wakefield. Here an Altofts family stand in front of one of the cottages.

Old Normanton around the church, the old village's centre. Normanton Hall is at the extreme right; it was demolished to make way for the church school. Note the young boys drinking from the village pump.

This was part of old Normanton which stood on the site of what is now the police station. Note the thatch on the roofs on the cottages. These cottages stood until early in the twentieth century. Nearby were the village cross, smithy and village pond.

Prior to the arrival of the railways the major source of employment in the area was the land. Here the Eccles family of Altofts prepares to cut the hay in their fields. Mr Eccles sits on the hay cutter with Joe next to him. Also shown are George Eccles, Bryan Turton holding the rabbit and Mr Mauldini.

Gathering the hay was important to ensure the farm's livestock had feed during the winter. Here David Bains stands in front of a full load.

The Foxholes Farm team stand ready to lift and stack the corn in 1922. Once all the corn had been stacked the farmers and their farm hands usually helped other local farmers.

A team of men and their steam threshing engines toured the area, farm by farm. Here Albert Fearnley operates the steam threshing engine at Foxholes Farm. Once all the local farms had got their harvest in the village celebrated with Maypole dancing on the green near what is now the Robin Hood public house.

Altofts Lodge dates back to the sixteenth century. It was once one of a circle of houses that stood on the roads into Newland hall Estate. The wealthy families who lived there in the nineteenth century often opened their grounds for the children of upper Altofts.

William and Ann Ratcliff in their Sunday best. These outfits were very much the fashion of the area in the middle to late nineteenth century and on into the Edwardian period. The dark clothes were better able to cope with the soot from the thousands of coal fires in the towns.

This postcard shows Normanton Market Place around 1900. Note Young's haberdashery store on the right: this burnt down in 1938. Scarr and Sons' shop is next on the right. There is a cobbled path running right to left across the muddy market place and a complete absence of tram lines.

The tramway from Pontefract via Castleford to Normanton was constructed in 1905/06. Here the tram waits in High Street while local tradesmen are given the opportunity of the first run. Many local people attended this opening and gave them a hearty send-off.

J. Horn had a bakery near the Union Hotel, Castleford Road, at the start of the twentieth century. He supplied local shops with bread and cakes for many years, just one of the many suppliers who toured the area with their products.

A 1920s view of High Street. Note the baths building, completed on 26 March 1926, the year the trams stopped. The houses and shops on the left have since gone, and the former Majestic Cinema is now a council garage on the right.

Was this really the last tram car from Normanton? History tells a different story of dwindling numbers using the trams, as they faced competition from the buses.

A view in the 1960s of Wakefield Road before the turn into Market Street. The shops on the left were among the first to be built in Normanton; they served the railway station workers who were housed there. All have now disappeared.

These cottages were built by the railway companies in the 1840s for their workers servicing the needs of the station. This was new Normanton, away from old Normanton grouped around the church. The houses survived until a few years ago. Note the old Station Hotel in the background.

These railway workers' cottages stood on Market Street. Between these and old Normanton there was for many years an open space containing the village pond. On this open space the travelling shows of the day would perform for the people of the town.

Between the two public houses, the Crown (right) and the Royal Sovereign (left), stands a row of slightly superior railway houses that were built for the middle management at the station. Most of the senior managers' homes were on Station Road at Leebrigg.

Another 1960s view of Wakefield Road. These houses eventually joined the mining communities at St John's and Woodhouse to the railway workers' community. All that now remains is the Methodist chapel, built in 1874, at the top of the hill.

Altofts has also changed. The graveyard at Normanton parish church could no longer cope with the deaths in the middle to late nineteenth century. One child in every five died before reaching five years of age. The Altofts cemetery was opened in 1879 and contained two mortuary chapels; this war memorial was added after the First World War.

Looking down Church Road, Altofts. The Horse and Jockey public house is almost certainly the oldest pub in the town. It was described in its sale document in 1881 as an old-established ale house.

The vicarage in Altofts was built in the 1870s to house the priest at the new Altofts parish church next door. It now forms part of a residential home.

This cottage, with the Stringer family standing in front, was one of a number that were spaced along Church Road. For many years they formed a loose link between Pope and Pearson colliery village at Low Altofts and the homes of the station staff at Leebrigg.

The Lord Nelson public house stood on an area of land between the canal and river at Altofts. Thousands would gather there at weekends. The owner demanded that the Aire and Calder Navigation remove its horses stabled there. The canal company then said that if they could not use the stables, the bridges over the canal would be of no use to them, so they removed them. No one could get to the now-deserted Lord Nelson and the owner subsequently went bankrupt.

This tram is coming down Castleford Road on this pre-1926 postcard. The building on the right was the Primitive Methodist chapel. Note the carriage behind the two boys on the left.

The trams could not compete with the buses that began to appear in the 1910s. Gillard's bus company served the town for many years. It was a very popular choice for many Normanton people on an excursion to the coast or countryside, as seen here in the 1960s.

The buses soon developed a service to all parts of the district. However, the local people had to get accustomed to this new form of transport. Young Rosie Gillot, seen here (standing), was one of the buses' first victims, killed in the 1920s in a road accident.

This early B&S bus waits for its passengers in the market place in the 1920s. Young's shop behind is advertising a range of clothes for both sexes plus carpets, floorcloths and linoleum. In front of the old police station at the extreme right is a tram.

The market place in the 1950s. At the extreme right is the entrance to Normanton's 'Public Market'. A parade of small shops selling a variety of goods leads to the open market behind.

The Fox public house stood for many years at the bottom of Foxholes Lane next to the canal. It served the needs of the many boatmen who tied up nearby to await their barges being filled with coal from the Fox pit and then the drift mine that replaced it.

Colin Heald and his father sit on the grass in front of one of Normanton's brickworks in the 1940s. This was was located at Newland Lane end and survived until the turn of the twenty-first century. The brickyard left at Altofts is now the only one in the country that still makes the larger, once common bricks.

Normanton has been served well by its own fire brigade since this second-hand steam-driven appliance was purchased by Normanton Board in 1910 for £180.

Normanton's first steam-driven fire appliance in action in Woodhouse Mount against a fire at the Hark to Mopsey public house.

A more modern fire appliance fights the fire that partially destroyed the headmaster's study, the general office and four classrooms of the former Normanton Grammar School, on 22 April 1977. This is now called Town Middle School.

Miss D. Higgins, Miss F. Hicks, Mrs Hicks, Mrs Johnson and Miss Greening celebrate Alexander Day, 18 July 1914.

As many and more modern motor cycles and cars start using the Normanton roads, the council had to make them useable all the year round. Here an early tar-laying machine transforms the once muddy roads.

For over 100 years Normanton roads had a surface of mud and muck and the horse and carriage struggled through. But the early motor cars and motor bikes could only use the roads when the mud had dried up in the summer.

This aerial view of Stanley Ferry shows an inlet, now filled in, to the left of the viaduct. 'Tom Puddings' were pulled out of the canal here, placed on a bogie and hauled by steam engine to and from the nearby St John's Colliery, where they were filled with coal.

Normanton has never had a Conservative MP. These Normanton Conservatives, including Mrs Denison and Stephen White, pictured here in 1940, no doubt hoped that this one day would change.

Many local industries were developed to supply the massive local collieries; one of these was the Detonator Company. Here we see some of its workers including Mary Flynn Smith, Emmie Beaumont, Nellie Sambrook, Bessie Charlton, Miss Pugh and D. Hurley.

This twin-engined Avro landed at the side of the Newland Lane railway bridge in 1949. Many children had never seen an aeroplane, so schools took the opportunity to show their pupils. Here a class from Queen's Street School, including (fifth from the right) Carol Slater, surveys the scene.

The wing-tips of the Avro Anson aircraft were removed to allow it to use the local roads. Here, escorted by a police car, it passes along High Street.

Two
Religion and Recreation

The only church in the Normanton area for many hundreds of years was the parish church. However, the people flooding into Normanton in the mid to late nineteenth century brought a need for other religious establishments. Early services were held in homes or small buildings, throughout the towns. As the people's individual wealth grew so did their desire to build churches and chapels. By the end of the century most religious organizations were represented in buildings. Once these had been built, finance was raised to build meeting rooms. These were used for Sunday schools and meetings, including recreation for the young. Each held a feast day every year to which the whole town looked forward, and joined in.

Dodsworth church was built to serve the Church of England population in the Woodhouse and St John Terrace area. These could not be accommodated in the parish church so a similar one was built at Hopetown.

A wedding in the Altofts Low End chapel. At one stage in its life it was called the 'Golden Dumpling'; it served the West Riding Colliery village community.

Altofts church May Queen attendants in 1941. From left to right, back row: C. Ryder, J. Thomas, D. Lowe. Middle row: ? Ryder, M. Ward, M. Shinkfield, S. Burley. Front row: D. Thornley, M. Thomas, D. Higging, E. Larter.

A good crop of food on the local farms was crucial for the well-being of the town. Each religious organization held its own festival to celebrate the harvest. Here we see the altar of the Methodist church during the Harvest Festival.

The Methodist church choir, winners of Castleford Eisteddfod. From left to right, back row: Harry Womack, George Dixon, Wendy Hall, Betty Holmes, Betty Bloor, Betty Wainwright, Helen Carter, Rita Kitton, Brenda Bache. Third row: Maureen Beedle, Noreen Smith, Jean Morton, Winifred Smith, Dorothy Beedle, Doris Dixon, M. Floyd, Revd Campton Wright. Second row: Pat Holt, Joan Kiddle, Valarie Wallace, Hazel Sanderson, Anne Goodlad, Joyce Holmes. Front row: Dorothy Martin, Pauline Lee, Judith Wallace, Paul Shearn.

A Methodist church concert party. From left to right, back row: -?-, Mrs Knowles, -?-, Mrs Borrill. Front row: -?-, Mary Oakley, Mrs Guy, Mrs Bradley, -?-, Doris Oakley, -?-, Mrs Prentice.

Methodist church May Queen, Denise Lythe, surrounded by her attendants, Les Womack, Joyce Smith, Audrey Hall, Margaret Kirk, ? Lythe, Monica Durkin, Audrey Kirk, Poppy Addy, Jean Prentice, M. Knowles, Billy Churchill, Eileen Hall, Lily Churchill, Raymond Durbin, Dorothy Durbin, Keneth Wandless, Dorothy Partridge, Winnie Cookson, Dorothy Skidmore, Irene Limb, Pat Holt, Trevor ?, Grace Skidmore, Margaret Whittington, Margaret Durbin, Margaret Holmes, Betty Limb, Wendy Hall and Mary Lythe.

Cushion Bearer Margaret Butler leads the Methodist church's first May Queen, Jean Harrison, and her attendants, Rita Woodcock (left) and Maureen Appleyard (right) through the Methodist church.

The Methodist church, like all other religious organizations in the town, organized many different activities for its members. The number of young people frequenting the Methodist church can be judged by the size of its Scout group in 1955.

Father Herfkins was Normanton's first Roman Catholic priest since the sixteenth century. When he came to the town in 1885 after working in Dewsbury, the local Catholics had no church. By the time of his death in 1911 aged sixty-seven, the Catholic community had a church, a school, a presbytery and a working men's club. Here his funeral cortège passes the 'broad flags'.

The Roman Catholic Children of Mary procession through Normanton. In the centre is C. Hughes and at the extreme right is Anne Cunningham.

This gathering of the Children of Mary was at another date and includes, from left to right: -?-, M. Hughes, N. Fabel, -?-, M. McQuire, -?-, H. Roche, -?-, M. Neary.

St John's School first Holy Communion, 1959. From left to right, back row: Mr J. Ray, -?-, ? Sullivan, D. Palmer, S. Carby, -?-, J. Gallagher, -?-, -?-, T. McDermott, M. O'Hara, -?-, J. Nelson, -?-, -?-, S. Jackson, Canon O'Grady. Middle row: J. O'Hara, -?-, -?-, J. Gill, -?-, A. Booth, P. Wilkinson, S. Shaw, -?-, -?-. Front row: -?-, S. Mitchell, E. Clarke, K. Appleyard, Mrs Stanton, -?-, -?-, -?-, A. Wrozek, -?-, -?-.

Canon O'Grady with teachers Mr G. Ray, Mrs A. Stanton and Miss M. Bubb preparing the children in this group for Holy Communion in 1959.

Normanton Parish church choirboys in 1950. From left to right, back row: Gerald Stevenson, Alf Bellwood, Bob Benson, Stuart Sadler, Arnold Jones. Middle row: Geoff Stevenson, Joseph Harper, ? Bushby, Malcolm Hartshorne. Front row: David Parkinson, Bob Abson.

Each religious organization had its own day to parade through the town, while the rest of the town watched. This was usually followed by a carnival. Here is the parish church carnival in 1945. Second from the right is Anne Bird.

Normanton parish church Cub Scouts, 1951. From left to right, back row: Jim Bird, Malcolm Marsh, Brian Dodd. Middle row: Christopher Stones, Terry Cadman, Derek Govan, ? Cadman, Graham Rhodes. Front Row: Derek Stokes, Rodney Smith, ? Dodd, -?-, Peter Riding, David Parkinson.

Among the organizations using the various meeting rooms in the twentieth century were the Scouts and Guides. Here the Guides are presented to the Mayor and his wife, Mr and Mrs Mackinnon, outside Normanton Town Hall. They include Margaret Butler and Norah Hazelden.

A procession leaves the churchyard and, with the police leading, sets off up Snydale Road. The man with the umbrella, centre right, is Albert Roberts, Normanton's MP at this time. The old cottages behind had stood for many centuries but were later pulled down to provide a car park.

Normanton Operatic Society grew out of the choirs that were established by the religious organizations. The society is represented here by its women members. From left to right, back row: -?-, Kathy Ferguson, -?-, Sandra James, Bevery Kappes. Front row: -?-, Alma Nicholson, Barbara Burgess, Elsie Blankley, Sheila Tomlinson, -?-.

The men of Normanton Operatic Society. From left to right, back row: Jack Robert, David Hartill, Clarry Blades, Jack Preston, Tony Layden, Peter Glover, Tony Lancaster. Front row: Raymond Caston, Billy Marsh, Stan Parkinson, Gwynn Stevens, Jim Burgess, Gary Davies, John Knappes.

St John's Terrace was the colliery housing for the nearby St John's Colliery at Newland. Everyone knew where you were going as you walked down the street to the toilets with an old newspaper. The privies were a later addition to the estate and were located at the bottom of each street.

The estate had shops, a Working Men's Club and rugby and football teams. Here a group, including Mrs Knee and John and Stephen Booth, celebrate Coronation Day in 1953 with a street party in St John's Street.

Residents of Prospect Avenue also celebrated the 1953 Coronation. From left to right, back row: Leo Dalton, Dennis Auty. Middle row: -?-, Shirley Trevis, Jacky Myers, Doreen Dalton, Derek Auty. Front row: Barbara Jolley, Bernard Armitage, Lorraine West.

Before street parties, parents would make all the food and organize games so the children had a day to remember. A quieter, more relaxed celebration was held by the parents later at night.

Another group celebrating Coronation Day in 1953. From left to right: G. Kirk, A. Mathews, Marlene Townend, John Hanscombe, Dennis Mathews, Norman Lanley, Christine Morris, Mrs Morris, Joan Shaw, Joyce Marchant.

Most people who were young children at the time of the Coronation will never forget what they did that day. Every street had its party. This photograph of the Anson Avenue party will ensure these children do not forget.

The town enjoyed its many carnivals. This one passing down Castleford Road in 1930 includes Sylvia Batty, Gwen Stead, Freda Moorhouse, Minnie Bird and Dolly Jacobs.

The area needed little excuse at that time for many of its people to band together and arrange a carnival. The Festival of Britain in 1951 was another excuse. This is Mary Shinkfield on the Labour Party float.

Altofts West Riding Colliery Band in the 1920s. From left to right, back row: R. Marsden, R. Taffinder, A. Crossman, S. Frost, K. Cresswell, W. Bednall, ? Frost, W. Cresswell, S. Sykes (?). Middle row: A. Crossland Snr, C.J. Frost, B. Gibson, ? Dean, A. Forester, W. Flintoff, J. Dowton, C. Goldthorpe, J. Turner (secretary). Front row: J. Turner Jnr (kneeling), F.A. Blower, D. Limb, A. Cadman, I. Shepherd, M. Rowlands, T. Penny, A. Burton.

The earliest court case involving Altofts people recorded in the Wakefield Manor Court Rolls was when they chopped down a tree on a local estate. These Altofts children in 1934 are following a tradition in the village that must have lasted several hundred years. That tradition has now ceased.

For over seventy-five years Altofts had its carnival day which provided sports and entertainment for all the family. Can you recognize any of these children who set out from the Silkstone building for the last Altofts Carnival in 1951?

The Avillions were a group of men and women who entertained the people of Normanton with songs and dances, all for charity. The men were, from left to right: Tom Megson, -?-, Chick Wilshire, Stan Bradley, -?-, Tom Hopson.

The following children were present in 1943 on HMS *Courageous*. From left to right, back row: G. Dunn, W. Stones, G. Addy, J. Banks. Front row: S. Walker, R. Trevis, J. Nicols, Margaret Sanderson, Doreen Bywater, Majorie Boulby, Hardwick, Eileen King, Atkinson, Margaret King.

Weddings always ensure a family gathering. In those days the couples' families all lived nearby, and a wedding like this of Mr Robinson and Miss Kaiser in 1922 was cause for extended entertainment.

A wedding on Normanton Common in 1910. From left to right, back row: Bert Davies (policeman) and his wife Ethel (the bride's sister), Fred Riley and Minnie Cheeseborough (the wedding couple), -?-, -?-. Front row: Ivy Nash, Ben Cheeseborough, Evelyn Nash.

Jack and Eva Chapman find other sources of entertainment as they take a ride on their dad's motorbike. This photograph was taken in Old Normanton, in a place called the Orchard, around 1926. The cottages were situated where Normanton Police station now stands.

This family group has gathered in 1955 to celebrate the fiftieth wedding anniversary of Elizabeth (Cissy) Mason, sitting in the centre. Behind the wall are, from left to right: Ena Jubb (*née* Mason), Charlie Alway, Madge Mason (?), Jack Mason, Sylvia Alway (*née* Mason), Marlene Townend, Ivy Sabey (*née* Mason), Bill Mason, -?-, Marion Mason. In front of the wall: Harold (Hag) Mason, Roger Sabey, David Alway, Alan Mason, Kath Jubb, Alf Sabey.

As the wealth of Normanton people grew, they were able to have days at the coast. Ladies' bathing costumes slowly grew smaller. These bathing belles at Blackpool showing off the fashions of the 1930s are, from left to right, Mrs Turner, Mrs Hughes and Mrs Rushton.

In the mid to late nineteenth century, families often had little to celebrate, as one in five young children died. The first priority was clean drinking water and a good sewerage system, and as the town's wealth increased so did the health of its residents. By the early twentieth century a baby clinic had been established; here we see a group at the clinic in 1937, including G. Pugh.

The Williams children including 'Mary and the twinees', who, from the looks on their faces, did not enjoy this experience. They lived in Mopsey Square, directly behind the Hark to Mopsey public house.

Three
Education

The great majority of people who came to Normanton in its boom period from 1840 to 1870 could not read or write. Initially the collieries set up their own schools in the colliery villages for the children of their workers. Raising finance to build schools was a major problem for the town's board and religious organizations. The majority of those schools still stand to day, although they are not all still used as schools.

A group of Normanton teachers pose during the Boer War in 1899. At the right on the bottom row is Ethel Cressey (*née* Jackson); third from the right on the same row is S.B. Woodhead. Mrs Tomlinson is also present.

Altofts Colliery School, Standard III, 1910. From left to right, back row: Mrs Adcock, A. Webster, H. Megson, W. Gibbons, H. Bradley, G. Glen, A. Measham, I. Shepherd, R. Toon, C. Stone, W. Pritchard, B. Doody, J. Gillard, Mr T. Goodhall. Third row: C. Teasdale, F. Allen, W. Burr, W. Hope, H. Cranswich, J. Armstrong, W. Roscoe, W. Johnson, T. Reed, M. Plant, J. Slatter, T. Whalton. Second row: A. White, G. Beard More, S. Timmins, B. Colwood, A. Armstrong, F. Webb, J. Doody, B. Whittingham, I. Allen, D. Glassard, L. Burton, J. Cowley. Front row: L. Webb, G. Harris, E. Greenhalsh, E. Plant, E. Hopson, J. Benton, A.Q. Briggs, L. Thompson, E. Clark, J. Brook, W. Grady, L. Holmes. Sitting at the front are E. Woodcock (left) and B. Powell (right).

Altofts had two schools; the National School is seen here in 1890.

Altofts National School in the early 1900s, Second from the left on the back row is Marjorie (Madge) Ann Kniveton (born 1897, died 1975).

Altofts National school in 1910. Included are: H.M. Dyson, M.A. Pickens, A. Pearson, D. Smith, R. Master, M. Kitcher, S.A. Carter, S. Hoyle, H. Toddington, D. Paley, D. Vennart, L. Chafer, W. Marshall, S. Elliot.

Martin Frobisher School, formerly Altofts National School, in 1957. From left to right, back row, Fletcher (X), Salmon, -?-, Hepworth. Middle row: -?-, -?-, -?-, -?-, -?-, Elaine Holt, Ann Sharpe. Front row: -?-, Smith, -?-, Dean, T. Bubb, -?-, Carter. Sitting: -?-, Sandra Meade, Ann Burgess.

The other Altofts school was financed by the Colliery. This colliery school class in 1932 shows the headmaster Tom Goodhall, and amongst the children are I. Woolley, Alan Richards, Beatrice Gibbons, Marjorie Wilkinson, Ron Brooke and A. Megson.

Loscoe was an area just outside Normanton, towards Featherstone. However, most of the children at the school came from Normanton. This class in the 1880s includes Mrs Cressey, third from the right on the middle row.

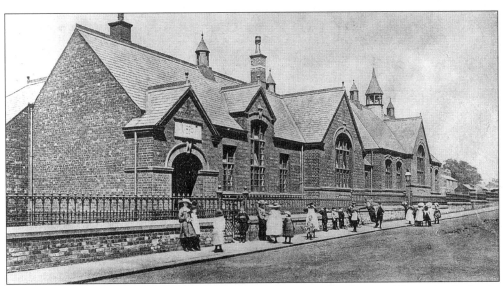

Under various Government Acts, Normanton was responsible for providing schools for its children. The board schools throughout the town were all built around the 1870s. This shows the Central Board School, Queen Street, part of which is now used as Normanton's Town Hall.

As the years passed, the title Central Board School was dropped and it came to be known as Queen Street School. This photograph shows the staff of the school in the 1950s, including Miss Eaton, Mrs Carrington and Mrs Williams.

The Central Board School in 1920. From left to right: D. Hirst, W. Hammond, D. Prentiss, E. Denis, E. Barber, Miss Brogden, E. Gregory, F. Rhodes, F. Richardson, A. Lily, N. Sykes, A. Earnshaw, J. Gregory, R. Green, F. Tiffany, Miss Wilson, E. Smith, P. Owen, W. Rigby, D. Hammond, A. Biggs, F. Snell, C. Bryant, ? Garfit, C. Barns, M. Weaver, P. Grainger, B. Lewis, M. Denison, A. Morris, K. Mackay, M. Dunford, V. Blankley, M. Barns, F. Davis.

The Normanton Common School was built to provide education for the children of the miners who worked at the Briggs Collieries at Whitwood. The school was rebuilt in the year 2000. This photograph from 1910 includes Eli Westwood, the boy in the centre of the front row.

Normanton Common became famous for its Bulb Days. In attendance in 1930 are, from left to right, back row: ? Bubb, B. Rawndon, E. Bennett, S. Jones, J. Williams, P. Hall, D. Toon. Front row: C. Adamson, J. Millington, E. Toon.

Normanton Common School Bulb Day, 1954. The teacher is Miss Binns and the children include Alan Mason, Margaret Jubb, David Sargent and Neil Hodgson.

Normanton Church School, 1951. From left to right, back row: -?-, ? Gullick, T. Bubb, -?-, S. Pickering, -?-. Middle row: ? Simeon, -?-, V. Metcalf, ? Watson, -?-, M. Jolliffe. Front row: ? Fellows, -?-, -?-, ? Hanscombe, S. Binns, ? Newton, Sitting at the right is Dodds.

Woodhouse School was another former board school named after the small hamlet that existed here. At playtime this day in 1956 are, on the see-saw, Glenis Phelps, Denise Bettley and Sheila Moss.

Woodhouse School in 1957. From left to right: -?-, John Robinson, -?-, -?-, Dennis Briggs, Brian Sandem, George Reed, Marie Churms, Susan Pallister, -?-, -?-, Denis Beckley, -?-, Linda Currey, -?-, Susan Teasdale, Jean Norton, -?-, -?-, -?-, Sheila Moss, Carol Barraclough, -?-, Pam Sharp, -?-, -?-, Eric Potts, Graham Crew, -?-, ? Jones, John Price, -?-.

Sports day was always the opportunity for the children to show their prowess. This Common School sports day in June 1956 took place in Morrison Fields. Note Good Hope Row in the background.

The Grammar School, Normanton

A committee was set up in August 1891 to re-establish a grammar school. They had funds available from the seventeenth-century will of John Freeston, and also £1,000 recently bequeathed by Thomas Ward. Local donations raised an additional £2,000.

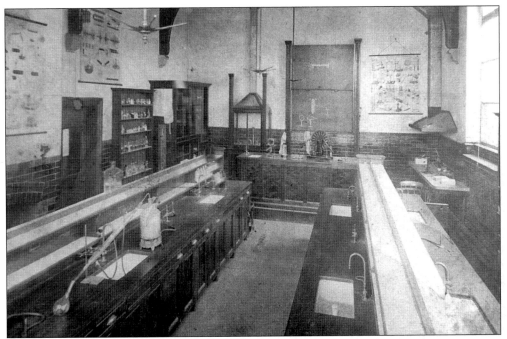

The school was built on a area of land in the town called Mill Flat Field. Three acres were purchased for £750 from the vicar of Normanton. This photograph shows one of the three classrooms at the school at that time.

The school was completed by 1897, at a total cost of £3,500. Mr C.W. Atkinson was the first headmaster. In 1905 it was enlarged; that year Mr C.E. Brittian became head when Mr Atkinson moved to another post.

Normanton Grammar School teachers. From left to right, back row: E.B. Haslam, -?-, -?-, -?-, J. Harries, A. Hall, A. Laycock, A. Lindop, E. Edmonds. Front row: A. Richardson, J. Musgrave, -?-, A.J.L. Durham, Mr Holden (headmaster), -?-, T. Houghton, B. White, S. Green.

Young ladies of Leebrigg School prior to a sports session. From left to right, back row: -?-, F. Jackson, P. Fisher, A. Littlewood, R. Fisher, Mrs B. Frost, P. Jowett, M. Megson. Front row: J. Bednall, M. Plank, A. Seal, M. Preston, J. Glazard, B. Glazard, ? Woodlock, M. Downton.

This kindergarten was started in Queen Street in 1908 for the young children of the more wealthy families of Normanton. It moved to the Normanton High School premises in 1912.

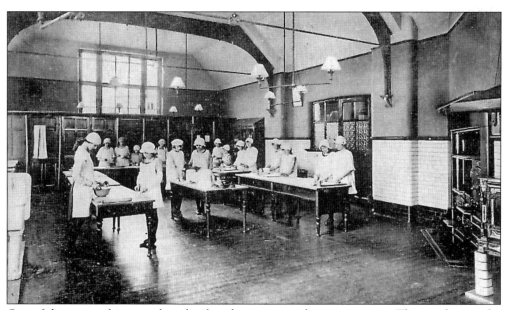

One of the main subjects at the school at that time was domestic science. This emphasizes the role of women at that period. Here we see the facilities to teach it at the High School. Miss Chambers was the first headmistress.

Normanton High School gymnasium. Many of the people of Normanton at that time could not read or write. The upstairs rooms were used for Normanton Technical College, where in the evenings the local adults, mostly miners, improved their education.

Normanton Girls' High School at a later date. From left to right, back row: ? Sheldrake, M. Holmes, ? Leake, A. Poundall, M. Benson, M. Rodway. Front row: J. Roberts, S. Townend, Miss Brook, B. Gawthorpe, -?-, A. Burton.

Normanton High School Seniors, 1927/28. From left to right, back row: J. Iveson, J. Thompson, M. Lee, H. Leake, B. Lockwood, M. Stokes, M. Holland, K. Walker, M. Carter. Middle row: J. Coombes, H. Adams, G. Malcolm, M. Massey, B. Davies, M. Shaw, J. Hall, J. Smith. Front row: S. White, A. Haslam, C. Williams, Miss Barron, C. Busby, -?-, M. Gibson.

Normanton High School, 1957/58. From left to right, back row: -?-, Diane Cable, -?-, -?-, Christine Worth, -?-, Susan Prince, Sandra Lynch, Janet Wheeler. Middle row: Jennifer Woolley, -?-, Wendy Odling, -?-, Jenifer Bilton, Carol Bloor, Carol Slater. Front row: Elaine Grice, ? Horn, Christine Smith, -?-, -?-, Miss Lavender, -?-, -?-, -?-, -?-, ? Moor.

Normanton Modern School camp in 1956. From left to right, back row: Colin Woodfine, Mr W. White, -?-. Front row: -?-, Gordon Appleyard, ? Sykes, Bill Bullough.

Normanton Modern School on holiday at Filey in the 1950s. From left to right, back row: Mr Carey, Mr White, -?-, -?-, E. Dukes, -?-, D. Hands, S. Taylor, Miss Thomas, Miss Bingham. From row: -?-, M. Wood, -?-, J. Bird, B. Abbot, M. Birchall.

Normanton Modern teachers, 1950s. From left to right, back row: Mr Davis, Mr Hall, Mr Harrison, Mr Marshall, Mr Knee, Mr Woodlock, Mr Hardcastle, Mr Jones. Middle row: Mr Gilby, -?-, Mrs Walker, Mrs Knee, Miss Sedgewick, -?-, Miss Burrows, Miss Jollife, Mrs Carey, Mrs Wray, Mr Stubb. Front row: -?-, Mrs Burgess, Miss Bingham, Miss Goodhall, Mr Pennington, Mr Burgess, Mr Beedle, Mr Carey, Mr Wilson.

Normanton Modern School, 1956. Rear row, from the left: third is Mike Diamond; fifth Alan Hurst; sixth Ian Vaughan. Third row, first from the left: Tony Hould; seventh Sheila Vause. Second row, sixth from the left: D. Prichard. Front row, third from the left: Terry Best.

Leebrigg School, now a junior school, was formerly a secondary school. The teachers in 1961 were, from left to right, back row: Roy Schofield, Mr Wheeler, Mr Woodhall. Front row: -?-, Ms G. Hoyle, Mr Ashford (headmaster), Stella Schofield.

Normanton High School visit to the Festival of Britain Exhibition in Leeds, 1951. Included are Iris Derwich, Molly Fredwell, Isobel Singleton, Anne Dunford, Janet Senior and Marie Ledger.

Four
Normanton at War

The twentieth century saw 'total war': men fought and women worked hard to ensure their men had the weapons and food for war. They also looked after the wounded. Even children contributed to the war effort; by writing and sending items to their fathers or older brothers, they helped to keep morale high.

A rare photograph of women engaged in war work resting in their hostel after a day preparing ammunition. Mrs E. Poundhall is on the right, next to the large flowers.

Born in Altofts in the mid-sixteenth century, Sir Martin Frobisher was a vice-admiral during the battle against the Spanish Armada in 1588. During the battle he accused Sir Francis Drake of being a coward. For his part in the victory he was knighted.

Although small in population prior to 1850, Normanton/Altofts men took part in conflicts throughout the world. Here we see one local man in his dress uniform in the mid-nineteenth century.

The Hubble/Stead family provided soldiers for many army campaigns including the north-west frontier campaign in India and the Boer Wars. Here we see them wearing the orders of one of the many different societies that flourished in the town.

Sgt Harry Hubble served in the Boer War and the First World War. He was awarded the Military Medal in 1917.

The First World War started on 4 August 1914. The 2nd Battalion, The King's Own Yorkshire Light Infantry (KOYLI), marched to Normanton from Strenshall near York. They arrived in France on 16 August 1914.

The 2nd Battalion KOYLI arrived at Le Havre on 26 August 1914. They were given the order 'there will no retirement.' John Roland Mellor (seen here) and four other Normanton men died obeying that order.

In January 1915, the Normanton companies of the1st/4th KOYLI had a farewell dinner in the Town Club. For many it was their last dinner in Normanton.

Thousands of Normanton's men answered their country's call to arms. Many joined the same unit and friends in the same street served together. This postcard was delivered to many in those streets.

The town was so behind its men at the front that some of their children were dressed up as soldiers. Here stands George Parkinson in 1918.

By June 1915 over 1,500 Normanton men had volunteered, and local committees were raising money to help families of soldiers who had been killed. Harry Parkinson of the KOYLI was one of those killed.

The town's children were saving their pennies to send parcels to their fathers in the trenches. John Stead (on the right, with a friend) served with the KOYLI and was killed in the First World War.

William Gillot was another casualty of the war. On the back of this photograph someone has pointed out that William received a medal.

J.H. Gibbons, formerly of Pope and Pearsons Colliery, joined the Royal Navy. It must have been quite a contrast to working underground. Again, he lost his life in the conflict.

Thomas Slater (front right) during his training for war. I published this photograph in the *Wakefield Express* a few years ago and was contacted by his family who asked me for a copy as it was the only photograph they had seen of him with legs. He lost them during the war.

With all the men at the war, housing repairs were not being carried out. The result was that over 50 per cent of the houses in Woodhouse were classed as unfit to live in. Here Henry Lacy poses with his proud parents.

Here are R. Noon and family of St John's Terrace. The St John's Terrace houses were classed in 1915 by the town's Medical Officer 'as a standing disgrace'.

This is Harry Womack and a Serbian friend in 1916. Harry was awarded a silver medal and crown by HM King Peter I of Serbia in Salonica on Christmas Day 1916. He died in 1971 aged seventy-six.

The first battle of the Somme started on 1 July 1916. Hundreds of Normanton's men were killed or wounded on that day. Here are Tom Dinsdale (cap on) and Arthur Ellis (arms crossed).

Under orders to stay in three ranks as if on parade, they marched into the invisible scythes of the German machine guns, and were mown down. Here is Joseph Mason, KOYLI, with his wife in 1915.

It was intended that the infantry should punch a hole which the cavalry would drive through and end the war, but they stood no chance. Laurence Heald, a cavalryman, is seen here with Edith Brigg.

John Archibald Yates of the East Surrey Regiment fought in both world wars and died in 1972. By the time John volunteered, the authorities had realized that if local men were posted to the same unit they got killed together and the effect of so many telegrams arriving in one small area was not good for the morale of the town.

The Cox family and friends, during the First World War. From left to right, back row: Ernest Hartil, John Cox, Lewis Cox, Joseph Cox. Front row: Austin Cox, William Cox, Martin Cox.

Because continuous shellfire damaged the communication lines, flags had to be used for signalling at the front. Third from the right on the middle row is Willie Taylor.

While the men were ordered 'at all costs' to attack, their families waited for the telegrams of death. This is the Williams family, many of whom went to war.

Joby Williams, who watched the cavalry go into action. He remembered that 'they were almost wiped out' and of the Leeds Rifles, 'few staggered back'. He was involved at Ypres, where 'the whole place smelled of death'.

GOD SEND YOU BACK TO ME

God send you back to me, —
Over the mighty sea;
Dearest, I want you near.
God dwells above you,
Knows how I love you,
He will bring you back to me!

BY PERMISSION OF THE NEWMAN PUBLISHING CO. LTD., LONDON, W.
BAMFORTH COPYRIGHT

Love's Longing

On the back of this card, Joby Williams wrote: 'Dear, read these words; will they ever come true? How happy we shall be if they would.' Joby did not come back.

A Normanton man managed to get this through the censors: 'We have been in the trenches for 24 days. It rained all the time.' This is the Taylor family during the First World War: Willie, Edie, John and Lizzie.

'With your back to the wall each man must fight to the end.' The 1st/4th Battallion KOYLI incurred 526 casualties at Ypres in 1917. James Stringer (right) was awarded a military medal; he died in 1975.

The Hurley family sent several of its number to the front, including Sgt Jack Hurley , 2nd-Lt Albert Hurley and Capt. J. Hurley. Capt. Hurley, a former coal-face worker, was summoned to Buckingham Palace to receive the Military Medal while in hospital recovering from the effects of gas.

Hundreds of Normanton men died, and many were awarded high military decorations. On the left is Walter Gillott of the KOYLI.

Not many Normanton men were captured: they 'fought to the end'. On the back of this photograph of Bob Preston he notes that it was 'Whit Sunday in Prison, 1918'.

Fifth from the right on the middle row is Bob Brown, who fought with the International Brigade in the Spanish Civil War and then later volunteered for the Second World War.

Here we see Sergeant Major Bob Brown of the KOYLI, who survived both world wars, being presented to Princess Alexandra on her visit to Normanton. Mr and Mrs Mackinnon are in the centre.

Lt Irvine Richardson of King Street served with the Army in Africa and continued his degree course after the war in African languages. He later made expeditions into the African interior, wrote several books and lectured in African languages at London University.

Brigade sports day. From left to right, back row: Smith, Seal, Wilson, Hill, Millard, Edwards. Middle row: Austin, Todd, Parker, Stead. Front row (sitting): Finn, Loughton, Bowbanks.

K. Knowles lived in Queen Street. He was 6ft 4in tall and was accepted into the Navy under age. He served through the Second World War, during which time he had several ships sunk beneath him. However, he survived and lived until September 2000, aged eighty-six.

By the time of the Second World War, local men did not necessarily serve together, and the different nature of the fighting meant that fewer men died at the same time. However, George Cudworth was one of those killed.

To avoid enemy detection during their attacks British planes had to fly low. This presented risks: D. Douglas's aircraft hit a mountain in 1943.

Normanton men were involved in many different theatres of war and some, like Albert Bullen, were captured. He became a prisoner of war in Stalag 8 during the Second World War.

The Williams family, having lost men during the First World War, suffered again in the Second. J. Williams was one of those killed in the latter conflict.

Roy Douglas Fraser, the author's father, was a member of the Reconnaissance Corps, a forerunner of specialist units such as the SAS. He was killed in Tunisia during the North African campaign on 27 April 1943.

When the world wars were over, many Normanton men still made themselves available to fight in the conflicts that continued world wide. At the back are sergeants Masefield, Harry Armstrong and Clifford Sykes of the KOYLI, on the Annual Camp.

Five
Other Sports

Normanton Grammar School athletic team pose with a shield they have won. From left to right, back row: P. Bird, K. Stains, J. Chivers. Middle row: ? Curtis, F. Swallow, Mr Holden, Mr Hughes, R. Jones, W. Guy. Front row: J. Swain, R. Clark.

Grammar School teachers sit in the pavilion on the school sports field while the guest of honour presents the trophies. The teachers are, from left to right, Mr Swallow, a guest, Mr Holden, Mr Henson, Mr Hudson and Mr Tryon.

Many Normanton Grammar School athletics champions went on to represent their county. The champions for 1937, seen here, were Rhodes, Curtis and Cooper.

Grammar School athletes on the running track, 1957. This field was used by the grammar school for many years, but after the grammar school and modern school amalgamated, it has lain unused, waiting for its future to be decided.

Normanton Modern School athletic team gather round their javelin thrower in 1956. From left to right, back row: Margaret Evans, -?-, Sheila Vause, Sylvia Turner, Doreen Woodcock, -?-, -?-, -?-, -?-, -?-, Harold Robinson, -?-, Jim Sambrooke, Ken Williams. Front row: Mr Stubbs, Pat Morgan, -?-, Alan Beck, -?-, -?-.

Normanton Badminton Club, winners of the Castleford and District Badminton League in 1954. From left to right, back row: P. Haigh, P. Jones, G. Abbot (president), J. Sweeting. Middle row: B. Brown, J. Chivers, E. Gill, G. Eccles, T. Clarkson. Front row: B. Buttery, P. Buttery, J. Wilkinson, M. Sweeting, E. Brown.

For some, the height achieved in athletics was measured by a cane between two poles, shown here by Geoffrey Kniveton in the early twentieth century. Geoffrey eventually became Senior Master at Elland Grammar School.

Basketball flourished for a few years in the 1970s and '80s. This team, besides winning local leagues, reached the semi-final of the Yorkshire Cup. From left to right, back row: Josie Copley, Howard Firth, Vernon Copley, Reg Edwards, John Kilcommons, S. Chung, J. Jones. Front row: Roy Fraser, Andy Stuart, Alan Beckitt, Mick Beckitt. Mick Copley, Terry Lethbridge, Bryan Fraser.

Bowling is possibly the oldest sport in the area; it was being played at Altofts over 150 years ago. Here the Lower Altofts WMC bowling club team of 1931 show off their trophies. Included on the back row: ? Newton, J. Fish, J. Turner. Front row: Horace Megson (middle), Frank Megson (left).

The Commercial public house bowling club, 1935. From left to right, back row: L. Blackhorne, -?-, R. Blackhorne, Tolley, -?-, ? Dyson, J. Watson, -?-, Middle row: H. Childs, ? Burrows, ? Appleyard, A. Jones, J. Whittam, ? Barstow, V. Winfield. Front row: ? Beavors, L. Stuckey, B. Jones, H. Hall.

Many young men took up boxing as a means of supplementing the family income, and Normanton over the years has produced some fine boxers, including Dan Armstrong, seen here.

Boxing made a brief come-back at Sharlston in the 1970s and '80s. The club produced some fine boxers. Bryan Fraser, here officiating at this in-house bout, was a former army boxing champion; he was the co-founder and first secretary of the club.

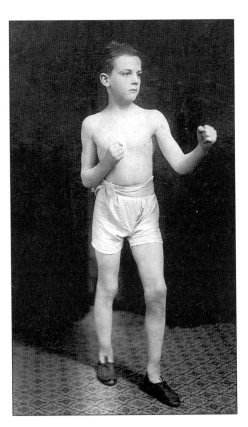

Many of those early boxers completed a shift in the pit before travelling by train to the venue of the fight. They slept on the train coming back and reported on time for the next day's shift. This is Jack Mason in 1933.

Altofts Primitive Methodists' cricket team. From left to right, back row: C. Kellett, ? Rarcliff, ? Kellet, M. Sykes, H. Ratcliffe, W. Ramsden, C. Ratcliffe. Front row: George Williams, Billy Williams, Ernest Kellet, Mark Sykes, Eddy Binns, -?-, J.W. Clark.

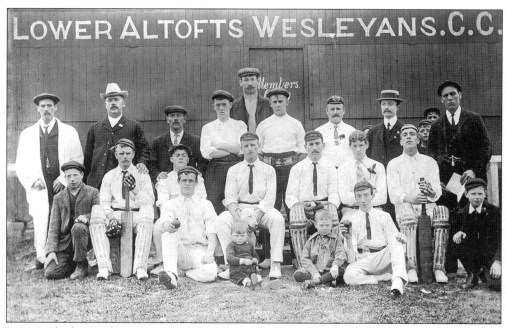

Lower Altofts Wesleyans' cricket club, 1920s. Included on the back row are T. Doody, ? Toddington, ? Stone and B. Penny, and S. Armstrong is on the middle row. On the floor are I. Dowton (left) and M. Brown(right).

Many cricket teams like this one from Park Avenue in the 1930s disappeared when the houses in the area were demolished.

Normanton Grammar School produced many teams over the years. From left to right, back row: Mr Bellamy, J.W. Holmes, Raines, Laycock, -?-, Haslam, -?-. Front row: Jackson, B. Cooke, Lamb, Gill, -?-.

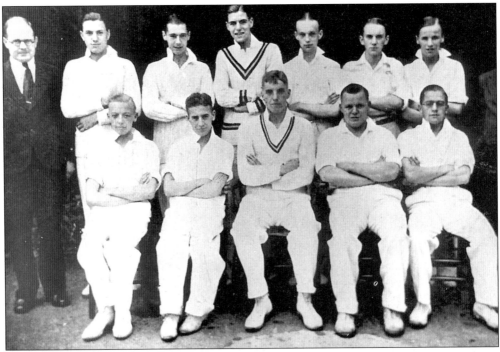

This Grammar School team includes, from left to right, back row: Mr Bellamy, J.W. Holmes, Hawes, Laycock, Haslam. Front row: Gill, Lamb, B. Brooke, Jackson.

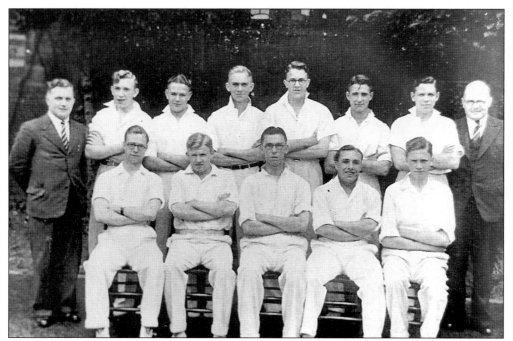

Normanton Grammar School cricket First XI in 1939. From left to right, back row: Mr Young, Wood, Teal, Downing, Dunmore, Atack, Cooper. Front row: Mr Bellamy, Hepworth, Edmonds, Westwood, Price, Midgley.

This Altofts cricket team includes Bob Deakin (front left), Jack Bednall and Henry Hall (extreme right).

Normanton's National Union of Railway workers' cricket team. From left to right, back row: -?-, A. Shepherd. Middle row: M. Limb, J. Rodney, -?-, Gothorpe, -?-, Howell, N. Hinchcliffe. Front row: J. Harlow Poole, Limb, Hincliffe (with shield), D. Allen.

Benson Lane cricket team in 1948. From left to right, back row: Jess Teace, Martin Kaye, Robinson, Alan Parkinson, Middle row, Bev Davies. Front row, Reg Rushton, Frank Sadler, Sam Jones, Ken Holmes. They scored the best win of the season, dismissing British Ropes for 14 runs.

Normanton's Mayor, Jim Kenny, presents Darts Panel winners' trophies to Hope Town WMC team, Frank Ellam, Ken Harold, Maurice Wood, Joe Bailey, John Fradgely, John Durkin, Frank Vause and Jim Durkin.

Normanton cycling club in 1937. Cycling for many was the only way to have a day in the country or at the coast, and cycling there and back with their friends was a social day out. Note the sidecar on the bicycle, centre left.

A Normanton fishing club. The first man on the left is Albert Watson; John Rafter is also featured.

Dr Alistair MacKensie, whose father was possibly Normanton's first doctor. They lived in the Orchard at Normanton. Alistair served in the Boer War and the First World War. He came to be regarded as the world's foremost designer of golf courses. Amongst the many hundreds he worked on was the Augusta National. He died in California in 1934 aged sixty-three.

Altofts (Leebrigg) School in 1961. From left to right, back row: Mr Ashford (head teacher), Val Thackray, Jean Keith, Kathleen Hardy, Mrs S. Schofield. Front row: Carol Hudson, Norma Brown, Ann Sharp, Christine Bryant, Jennifer Vine.

Altofts (Leebrigg) School Senior netball team, 1962. That year, they were winners of the Ben Bacon Trophy. From left to right, back row: Stella Schofield, S. Book, J. Vine, Mr Ashford (head teacher). Front row: V. Thackeray, C. Bryant, N. Brownson, J. Greatorex, K. Hardy.

Altofts (Leebrigg) School junior team in 1962. Beside Mrs Schofield and Mr Ashford are Judith Goodwin.

Altofts (Leebrigg) School netball team, 1977/78. They were winners of their section in the Castleford and District League. From left to right, back row: -?-, G. Ellis, S. Statham, J. Hancock, L. Auty. Front row: K. Ratcliff, C. Govan, S. Robinson (captain), S. Hall, J. Dyson.

Normanton High School netball team, 1924. From left to right, back row: A. Dunkley, L. Thorpe, M. Hudson. Front row: W. Jarvis, M. Newton, M. Eaton, Miss Griffiths.

Normanton High School netball team, 1928. The team includes Knappe, E. Senior, M. Shaw, D. Coe, D. Kiershaw, V. Jack.

Normanton High School annual staff *versus* pupils fixture, 1936. Those pictured include Wilma Harmar, Audrey Ward, Miss Harrison and Ms Armitage.

Normanton High School hockey team, 1924. From left to right, back row: W. Jarvis, A. Dunkley, M. Hudson, Miss Griffiths. Middle row: F. Blackburn, M. Eaton, M. Newton, D. Druce, D. Lodge. Front row: L. Thorpe (who later played hockey for Yorkshire), M. Shaw.

Hopetown pigeon club, winners of the Normanton Hospital Cup. Included are Mr J. Qualter, Mr Jenkins and Mr A. Jenkins.

Loscoe Board School rugby team in 1905, winners of the Yorkshire Cup. From left to right: D. Crew, J. Leake, A. Talbot, W. Leighton, J. Copeland, J. Sims, G. Fox, H. Lily, F. Shaw, A. Lily, W. Guest (captain), A. North, A. Wilkinson, F. Moore.

Normanton has always produced good rugby players. Some have represented their country, others have turned professional. These Modern School students, who represented Yorkshire, are Mick Stead, S. Carlton (captain) and Graham Blakeway.

Altofts Welfare tennis team, Winners of the Castleford and Pontefract District League, in the 1930s. G. Morrell, A. Summers, G. Knowles, A. Whittingham, S. Jackson, S. Hartley, E. Clark, J. Brabbon, A. Knowles.

Six

Football

Up to nationalization in 1947, the coal industry had suffered periodic depressions for over 100 years. Men would sometimes be lucky to be working two or three days a week. The Normanton area was predominantly dependent on mining for employment. Football enabled young men to keep fit for work, promoted team spirit and provided a spectacle for the less physically able. Teams represented different areas of the town and various organizations. Up to the 1960s, thousands watched those games.

Altofts Junior School must have been one of the first schools to win the Coal Owners' Shield. From left to right, back row: L. Slater, K. Brooks, H. Bennet, S. Statham, Flynne, I. Windross. Front row: S. Watton, J. Collinson, J. Smart, B. Winfield, C. Burrows.

Dodsworth School, 1924. From left to right, back row: E. Wilkinson, J. Crawshaw, J. Dyson, -?-, J. Booth, G. Lee, Mr Barnet. Front row: C. Feraby, J. Oldham, W. Smith, J. Bailey, H. Morley. Sitting on the floor: R. Spoford, G. Stanley.

Dodsworth School football team in 1947, winners of the Coal Owners' Shield and the Billy Empire Cup. From left to right, back row: B. Lister, K. Sykes, K. Middleton, K. Howell, C. Sherrat, B. Dye, T. Hatcher. Front row: White, R. Davies, J. Bailey, C. Dyson, L. Garner.

Leebrigg school football team, 1962/63, winners of the Coal Owners' Shield. From left to right: Mr Garfitt, N. Gooding, S. Triewsey, S. Handscombe, S. Yates, S. Beddard, Mr Hopwood, A. Close, F. Webb, S. Miree, G. Knowles, J. Whitely, A. Dean, D. Taylor.

Normanton Minor League team. From left to right, back row: H. Crossley, B. Gordon, Gordon, -?-, -?-, Mr S. Tomlinson, Mr F. Wilkinson. Front row: L. Bains, R. Bott, J. Morley, R. Marshall, R. Allchurch, B. Webb (who later joined Leeds United).

Woodhouse School team in 1950, with Mr Tomlinson and Mr Hardcastle. From left to right, back row: J. Wildey, P. Clarke, F.D. Jones, B. Box, A. Brighton, D. Miles. Front row: F. Kirton, L. Wilkinson, P. Lyons, G. Bales, N. Atkinson.

Loscoe Grove Board School team in 1904. From left to right, back row (trainers): F. Hutchinson, H. Savage, R. Rubery. Middle row (team): F. Fox, J. Leake, J. Sim, A. North, J.B. Talbot, G. Fox, A. Carter, H. Wright. Front row: A. Gregory, D. Crewe, C. Crewe, H. Crossley, H. Dodd, W. Guest, W. Leifgton, J. Copeland. Sitting on the floor: P. Mann, J. Griffiths.

Standing on the right at the back of this team in 1958 is Mr Freeston. From left to right, back row: D. Appleyard, G. Handscombe, -?-, Hughes, M. Bains. Middle row: G. Sandy, S. Severn, F. Hough, S. Smith, K. Webster. Front row: F. Smith, D. Lithgoe, P. Watson.

Normanton Grammar School team, 1919/20. From left to right, back row: J. Mills, A. Abbott, G. Hudson. Middle row: Guest, A. Greening, Heap, Hudson. Front row: H. Blakeley, S. Tomlinson, -?-, S. Barnet, Dolan.

Normanton Grammar School team, 1940/41. From left to right, back row: Mr Young, Mee, Speed, Briggs, Jordan, -?-, Westerman, Mr Tryon. Front row: Jackson, Ward, Downing (captain), Madely, Wilby.

Normanton Grammar School team, 1941/42. From left to right, back row: Mr Young, D. Williams, Armstrong, H. Jordan, C. Nightingale, Short, Bullock, Mr Banks. Front row: J. Wilby, W. Jackson, Briggs, A. Westerman, Atherton.

Normanton Grammar School team, 1951/52. From left to right, back row: Mr J. Beddows, A. Carr, P. Kirk, R. Harrison, -?-, Mr Holden (headmaster). Front row: -?-, D. York, D. Devey, D. Miles, J. Beddows Jnr.

In the years after the Second World War many short-lived teams were formed and then disappeared. This Rookery team, who played on a Normanton Park pitch, is seen in 1947 and includes C. Pugh, C. Douglas and C. Asquith.

An Altofts team in 1918. From left to right, back row: D. Dean, T. Richards, J. Thompson, A. Barstow, E. Bagnall, C. Whalley. Middle row: T. Brown, I. Cooper, W. Senior. Front row: T. Read, H. Megson, H. Rushton, C. Plimmer, H. Ruston, C. Schofield.

Altofts had an established football club in the 1870s. This team from 1922/23 is a direct descendant of that early foundation. From left to right, back row: Norris, Hobson, Barstow, Shilitoe, Bagnall, Senior. Middle row: Rains, Cooper, -?-, Teasdale, Schofield. Kneeling on the right: Rushton.

The Altofts team is claimed to be the oldest established club in the West Riding. Early teams played against the likes of Leeds United and Bradford City. From left to right, back row: -?-, Pickup, -?-, R. Measham, -?-, Jack Deakin, -?-, Jack Marsh. Front row: Eric Senior, Leslie Jones, Les Baines, -?-, -?-, Eric Jones.

Altofts team in the 1960s. From left to right, back row: Arthur Hardcastle, Lee Philips, Dean Powiss, Alex Scott, Tony Frost. Middle row: Eric Toddington, Keith Robinson, K. Phelps, Malcolm Shaw. Front row: Mick Cooney, Martin Bedale (mascot), Roy Schofield.

Rivalry between the various town teams was very keen. In 1931/32 this Hopetown team secured all the trophies. On the right of the back row are E. Higgins, Newell and H. Pell. The front row includes A. Webb (centre) and B. Newell (right).

Hopetown Juniors show off their cup in 1918/19. Third from the right on the back row is T. Carter. Sitting on the right is Whittingham.

St John's Wednesday during a successful year. From left to right, back row: Bill Dyson, -?-, Fred Johnson (goalkeeper), H. Williams, Holdsworth. Middle row: Joe Harper, E. Lee, Bob Webb, -?-, Hag Mason. Front row: T. Garner, Prop Reed.

This St John's Terrace ladies' team played to raise money for the many striking miners during the National Strike in 1926. From left to right, back row: Bill Horrace, Alice Watson, Jobb Williams, -?-, Jinny Bradley (goalkeeper), Booth, Agnes Jennings, -?-, -?-, Elsie Dyson. Front row: Agnes Jones, Elizabeth Riley, -?-, Helen Watson Smith, Julie Golding, John Lee.

St John's AFC was first formed in 1928 and was originally known as Normanton CYMS. This team of 1948 includes, from left to right, back row: -?-, -?-, George Golding, -?-, A. Beards, Stan Bradley (goalkeeper), Sid Wells, -?-, -?-, -?-. Front row: Colin Pugh, Swift, Howard Newsome, Trevor Thatcher, Ike Taylor, Alan Parkinson, George Stackhouse.

Whitwood, 1924. From left to right, back row: Mr A. Lilley, T. Ellis, B. Thornton, H. Errington, J. Carr, T. Jarret, F. Booth, Mr Holland, ? Ellis, E. Marchant, A. Senior, S. Pickles, S. Tolsdon, L. Farren, H. Stephens.

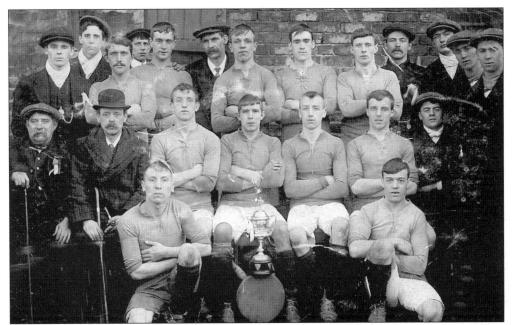

Altofts West Riding Colliery (Silkstone Buildings) team. From left to right, back row: Tomlinson, Webb, -?-, T. Williams. Middle row: Cooper, -?-, Dunn, S. Armstrong. Front row: -?-, Watton.

Altofts West Riding Colliery team. From left to right, back row: M. Brown, T. Brown, Hutchinson, J. Reed, E. Best, H. Jones, J. Hudson. Front row: A. Whittingham, -?-, J. Deakin, -?-, A. Hardcastle.

Altofts colliery team, 1919/20. From left to right, back row: J. Bagnall, A. Kirk, A. Bastow. Middle row: W. Senior, T. Brown, T. Hudson, I. Cooper. Front row: R. Schofield, H. Rushton, C. Haycock, S. Armstrong, W. Bains.

Silkstone Rovers. From left to right, back row: K. Howell, G. Gorman, Price, B. Birchall, T. Lee, H. Thornley. Front row: F. Timmins, A. Tucker, R. Turner, D. Pumford, B. Crossley.

The name of this team is unknown. From left to right, back row: Bradley, J. Hudson, Hardcastle (goalkeeper), W. Tomlinson, -?-, R. Webb, D. Watton, J. Kirk. Front row: J. Ward, -?-, C. Plant, H. Megson, -?-, C. Megson.

Benson Lane team, including Martin Mate, Jeff Davies, Jack Wilby, Reg Rushton, Jess Teace, Roy Gray, Ken Holmes, Peter Wilby, Vic Rushton.

Smirthwaite team, 1960/61. From left to right, back row: H. Parkinson, A. Parfitt, K. Allchurch, V. Woods, D. Batham, G. Pugh, C. Brain, C. Duffin, D. Cartwright. Front row: -?-, -?-, A. Scott, L. Brain, -?-, -?-, -?-, F. Barrett.

This Snydale team played in the semi-final of the Castleford and District Cup in 1998. From left to right, back row: Dick Longfield (coach), A. Smith (manager), Stuart Dale, Kris McTeague, Ian Carter, Peter King, Denis Price, Neil Kew, Luke Crossley, Michael Annington, Mark Westerman, Neil Chapman. Front row: Martin Elliott, Craig Millard, Lee Baddley, Chris Tonks, Stuart Carter, Danny Westerman, Kevin Sayce.